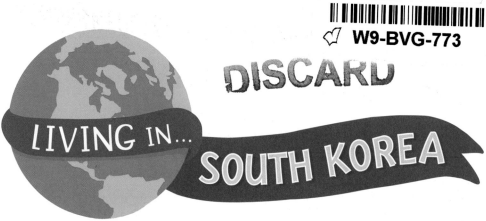

LIVING IN... SOUTH KOREA

by Chloe Perkins
illustrated by Tom Woolley

READY-TO-READ

SIMON SPOTLIGHT

An imprint of Simon & Schuster Children's Publishing Division • 1230 Avenue of the Americas, New York, New York 10020
This Simon Spotlight edition October 2017 • Text copyright © 2017 by Simon & Schuster, Inc. • Illustrations copyright © 2017 by Tom Woolley
All rights reserved, including the right of reproduction in whole or in part in any form. SIMON SPOTLIGHT, READY-TO-READ, and colophon are
registered trademarks of Simon & Schuster, Inc. For information about special discounts for bulk purchases,
please contact Simon & Schuster Special Sales at 1-866-506-1949 or business@simonandschuster.com.
Manufactured in the United States of America 0418 LAK • 2 4 6 8 10 9 7 5 3 • Library of Congress Cataloging-in-Publication Data
Names: Perkins, Chloe, author | Woolley, Tom, 1981- illustrator. Title: Living in ... South Korea / by Chloe Perkins ; illustrated by Tom Woolley.
Description: New York : Simon Spotlight, 2017. | Series: Living in ... | Series: Ready-to-read. Level two, Superstar reader. Identifiers: LCCN
2017007991 (print) | LCCN 2017014968 (ebook) | ISBN 9781534401440 (ebook) | ISBN 9781534401426 (paperback) | ISBN 9781534401433
(hardcover) Subjects: LCSH: Korea (South)—Juvenile literature. | BISAC: JUVENILE NONFICTION / Readers / Beginner. | JUVENILE NONFICTION /
People & Places / Asia. | JUVENILE NONFICTION / History / Asia. Classification: LCC DS907.4 (ebook) | LCC DS907.4 .P47 2017 (print) |
DDC 951.95—dc23 LC record available at https://lccn.loc.gov/2017007991

GLOSSARY

Baduk: a game between two people who place stonelike objects on a board in order to gain more territory from their opponent

Civics: the study of a person's rights and duties as a member of society

Historian: someone who studies or writes about past events and their meaning

Kingdom: an organized community or territory that is ruled by a king or queen

Peninsula: a piece of land surrounded by water on three sides

Republic: a form of government in which leaders are chosen or elected by the people

Soviet Union: a former country that extended from eastern Europe into northern Asia that broke up into Russia and fourteen other republics in 1991

Tae Kwon Do: a Korean martial art that emphasizes quick foot movements

Terrarium: a sealed, see-through container that holds plants

Water cycle: the continuous transformation of water from vapor to liquid, then back to vapor

Zone: an area separated or sectioned off from neighboring parts

NOTE TO READERS: Some of these words may have more than one definition. The definitions above are how these words are used in this book.

Annyeonghaseyo!
(say: ON-young-ha-say-yo) That's how
we say hello in South Korea.
My name is Min-jun.
I live in South Korea.
South Korea is a country
in Asia where more than
fifty million people
live . . . including me!

South Korea is part of the Korean Peninsula. The Yellow Sea is to the west, the East Sea is to the east, and the East China Sea is to the south.

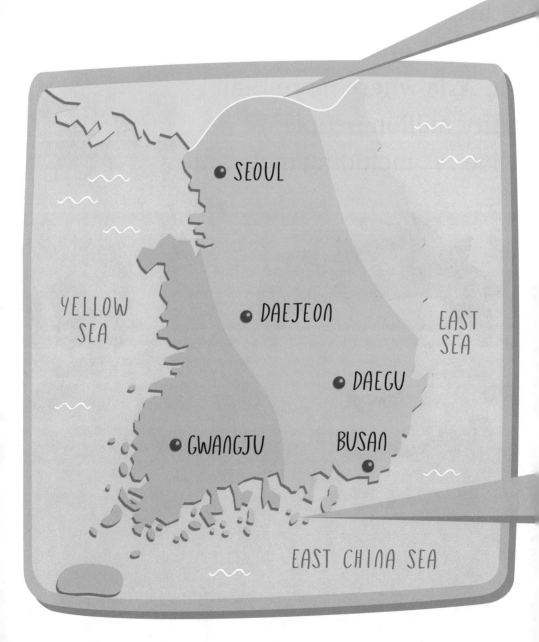

SEOUL

YELLOW
SEA

DAEJEON

EAST
SEA

DAEGU

GWANGJU

BUSAN

EAST CHINA SEA

To the north, South Korea borders the country of North Korea.

More than three thousand islands are part of South Korea too. Two of the islands have volcanoes.

Seventy percent of the land in South Korea is mountains. The Sobaek Mountains are in the south.

The biggest mountain range in the north is the T'aebaek Mountains.

I love going on vacation to the mountains with my family. Snowboarding is my favorite sport! There are lots of great places to ski and snowboard around Seoul.

SEOUL

Seoul is the capital and biggest city in South Korea. The city is more than two thousand years old!

INCHEON

Near Seoul is Incheon. Its busy harbor and transportation systems make the city a popular hub for business.

Many people call Busan the Summer Capital. This city is a great vacation spot with beautiful beaches.

Daegu is the center for fashion. People from all over the world come to this city for the Daegu Fashion Fair!

I live in an apartment in Seoul with my mom, dad, and twin brother, Ji-hu.

My parents both work
for a cell phone company.
They design programs that are
used in phones around the world!
Ji-hu likes to play baduk. Baduk is
a game of strategy. He is even on a
baduk team.

Each morning I wake up, take a shower, and get dressed. Then it is breakfast time.

We start with bean sprout soup. Next we eat white rice with steamed vegetables. Then our parents drive us to school on their way to work.

School starts at nine each morning. There are twenty-seven kids in our class. We learn Korean, math, English, civics, and science. Civics helps us understand our government and how to be good citizens.

We have a special visitor today.
She is a historian who studies
Korea's exciting past. Would you
like to hear about it?

People have been living in South Korea for more than ten thousand years. The first dwellers came from central Asia. Back then they adapted Chinese farming methods and a writing system based on Chinese characters. In the 1440s, King Sejong, the leader of the Joseon Dynasty, developed a new alphabet called hangul. It is still used today!

For centuries this land was populated by many small kingdoms. At times different kingdoms were in control. But in 668, for the first time, the whole Korean peninsula became unified under the Silla Kingdom.

Art and nature were highly respected
during this time. Artists would bring
themes of nature into their work,
whether it was fine gold jewelry or
simple pottery.

But by 935 the kingdom broke apart again. Over the next thousand years, rulers came and went. Some were from the peninsula. Some invaded from other countries. In 1910 Japan took control of the peninsula and would stay in charge until the end of World War II.

When Japan was defeated in the war, Korea was split into two zones. The United States of America controlled the south and the Soviet Union controlled the north. The two zones were supposed to be reunited.

Instead the Korean War broke out. It lasted from 1950 until 1953. Nothing was resolved. South Korea and North Korea are still divided today by a strip of land. It is two miles wide and cuts across the peninsula.

But in 1998 President Kim Dae Jung of South Korea started the Sunshine Policy because he wanted his country and North Korea to work together. In 2000 the leaders of the two countries met. In the years since, new leaders have not been able to settle the differences.

After our guest leaves, it is time for lunch! Today we are having kimchi bokkeum bap (say: KIM-chee bok-oom-bap). Kimchi bokkeum bap is fried rice and pickled vegetables. We also eat watermelon.

Next we go to science lab.
We are studying the water cycle.
Our class made terrariums!
We observe how temperature affects
water. The water cycle is very
important to South Korea's forests.

Every day I go to tae kwon do lessons after school. We jump and spin around. We learn how to control our movements. We are always kind and respectful to one another.

Back home Ji-hu
and I do our
homework.

Then it is time for dinner.
We eat beef-and-radish soup with rice.

After dinner Mom makes songpyeon
(say: SONG-pyun). Songpyeon are
rice cakes shaped like half-moons.
They are filled with sweet seeds, nuts,
or paste. Ji-hu and I help make them
for Chuseok (say: CHEW-sock)!

Chuseok is a harvest festival. No one works or goes to school. We celebrate it for three days every autumn when the moon is full. Tomorrow morning we will pay our respects to our ancestors.

We will also play games.

And then we will eat dinner with our family. We will have spicy soup, grilled meat, rice, and vegetable pancakes. And, of course, we will eat a lot of songpyeon!

Tonight, though, our parents surprise us with an early gift. We get a book about Olympic athletes from around the world. I love reading about all the athletes. My favorite chapter is about the winter sports.

I cannot wait for the Winter Olympics to come to South Korea. My family has tickets for the snowboarding event!

Maybe I will be in the Olympics someday! Would you like to visit South Korea?

ALL ABOUT
South Korea!

name: Republic of Korea (or South Korea for short!)

Population: 50.92 million

Capital: Seoul

Language: Korean, but most people in South Korea can also speak English, since it is taught in schools just like Min-jun's.

Total Area: 38,502 square miles

Government: presidential republic

Currency: won

Fun Fact: When babies are born in Korea they're immediately considered one year old!

Flag: White with a red-and-blue yin-yang symbol in the center, and each corner has a different symbol, called a trigram. White represents purity, blue represents negative forces, and red represents positive forces. Each trigram represents a different element, and together they symbolize harmony.